Volleyball Tips: Bite-Size Techniques to Boost Your Game

Ed Tennyson

Volleyball Tips: Bite-Size Techniques To Boost Your Game

ISBN-13: 978-1463660062

ISBN-10: 1463660065

PART 1

Volleyball Beginners' Drills

Volleyball Beginners' Drills

You've probably tried playing volleyball at some point in your life but then quickly gave up when you found it too difficult.

The truth is that volleyball isn't really that hard to master, especially since it deals mostly with repetition.

You just need to accept that you really have to start at the bottom, where skills are concerned and surely it can be quite frustrating, but just as with any other sport, practice DOES make perfect!

This means you'll just have to keep practicing your volleyball drills until you catch on and your game takes off.

Toss and Pass
This volleyball drill is done by two players.

One player tosses an easy ball and the other player passes it.

It would be best for you to do this drill at least 25 times and then switch roles with your partner.

Make sure that you focus on the proper passing and tossing technique as you perform each repetition.

You can expect the tossing and passing motion to become smoother as you become more comfortable with the drill.

Wall Hitting

This is one drill you can do alone because all you really need is a ball and a wall.

Pick a particular spot on the wall that you will hit.

Toss the ball to yourself and then swing to hit the exact spot on the wall that you choose earlier.

Timing is essential for this drill.

And you also have to make sure that you focus on executing the proper arm swing technique.

As soon as you get comfortable with the drill, take a few steps back and then go through the drill again.

This time, though, try to bring your arm high up in the air and attack the ball as you swing.

The primary benefit of this particular drill is that it allows you to work on strengthening and mastering your arm swing even without a partner.

Wall Blocks

Just like wall hitting, you can also perform this drill all by yourself as long as you have a wall to work on.

Begin by standing in front of the wall as if preparing to block.

Jump up and touch the wall as high up as you can, making sure you are in correct blocking form.

Get back to blocking position as soon as you hit the ground.

The purpose of this particular drill is to practice blocking with good form while staying away from the net.

You can ensure this by making sure that your arms do not scrape the wall when you jump.

One on One Setting

This drill comes in two variations.

The first requires just one player and a wall, whereas the other requires two players and a net.

If you choose to do the first variation, then you should set continuously to the wall.

But, if you have a partner who can go through the drill with you, then you can stand on opposite sides of the net and then set back and forth to each other.

The main benefit of this drill is to strengthen your hands and become more consistent in setting.

Remember that repetition is the key to improving your skills in volleyball.

Therefore, if you really want to become a good volleyball player, you'll have to go through the basic drills repeatedly until you master the game.

At first, you may find the drills tedious and a bit frustrating because of its repetitive nature, but when you start seeing improvements in your game, you will surely appreciate having spent the time and effort on your drills.

So, you see, learning how to play volleyball isn't really all that difficult.

It just needs a bit of time and consistent effort.

As long as you don't give up when the going gets tough, your skills will soon improve and in no time at all, you'll surely become a player any team can be proud to have.

Part 2
Fun Volleyball Drills

Fun Volleyball Drills

Most people who choose to play volleyball do so because they consider it a fun sport.

Although it is essentially a competition between two opposing teams, neither one of the competing teams would probably be into the sport unless they consider it a lot of fun.

But, learning how to play volleyball also entails a lot of hard work and some pretty tedious volleyball drills.

The best way for your team to learn the essential volleyball skills successfully is to use a set of fun volleyball drills.

By definition, drills are naturally difficult because they are designed specifically to help you master certain skills.

They can also become quite boring, which is a common reason for some players not really putting forth the necessary effort to perform drills properly.

Fortunately, some volleyball experts have developed a set of fun volleyball drills that are sure to encourage all team members to give it their all.

What better way to improve your skills than to have fun in the process, right?

Three-man Weave Drill
This is one fun drill that truly encourages teamwork.

It is performed by setting up three players in a triangular formation, with two in front and one at the back.

The player assigned at the back of the formation should stand about 10 feet behind the two other players.

Player A in front will then set the ball high up in the air and then Player C at the back positions himself under the ball and sets it to Player B.

The three players will then move in a counter-clockwise direction such that Player A takes the place of Player C and so on.

To make the drill more fun and interesting, the entire team can do it simultaneously in small groups.

You may set a punishment for any group that drops the ball and a reward for the last group standing.

Queen of the Court Drill

With this drill, groups of two, three, or four players are pitted against each other in a free ball play.

The first team to drop the ball loses.

The last team standing is then declared queen of the court.

All other teams must then go through a punishment and the winning team receives a reward.

This drill helps develop pride in the winning team and establish teamwork for those who have to go through the punishment together.

Volleyball drills really don't have to be tedious or boring.

There are effective ways of honing your skills in volleyball while still having fun.

One such skill you need to work on is that of diving to the floor for a deep dig.

While you may recognize the importance of this skill, you might get intimidated by the mere idea of diving to the floor to get the ball.

This is quite understandable, as most people who are learning how to play volleyball for the first time are naturally intimidated during the first few times that a game calls for them to make a deep dig.

One very effective way of honing your deep digging skill is to borrow a drill from football.

Here, you are made to run in place and then turn to a specific direction while continuing to run in place.

After several turns, your coach or trainer will blow his whistle, which is the cue for you to dive to the ground.

After a few times of doing this drill, you should no longer be quite as intimidated by a deep dig as you used to be.

To turn this into a fun drill, you can set consequences for the last person to hit the ground when the whistle blows.

This will cause you to hit the ground faster and often harder, which is very effective in eliminating whatever fears you may have of deep digs.

With the right amount of motivation and variation, fun volleyball drills can truly make training a lot easier and more enjoyable.

In fact, fun drills can be a lot more rewarding than traditional drills since it constantly reminds players that they are there because they enjoy the game.

Needless to say, any player who enjoys his sport will have a much bigger chance of becoming a great player than one who simply plays because he has to.

PART 3
The Importance of Tactical Drills

The Importance of Tactical Drills

Volleyball coaches often work on conditioning drills during off season.

At the beginning of the season, however, it is best to concentrate on technical drills.

And after the first few practices at the beginning of a season, it is best to start working on your tactical drills.

Tactical drills are the kind of drills that take all of the technical skills you have learned so far and then forming them into actual plays.

These drills will help develop teamwork and camaraderie in your team, as it teaches them to work together as one unit.

It also develops proficiency in the team, which gives you a sense of confidence that will surely help you in your games.

Among the most important aspects of tactical drills in volleyball are the development of trust among the team members and the teaching of players to work together as a strong and united team.

The drills allow the players to play off each other because they are confident that each of them will place the ball exactly where it needs to be on every single play.

To ensure that volleyball tactical drills are effective and successful, they have to be performed on a regular basis and repeated as often as necessary until each team member can finally perform his specific function as near perfection as possible.

The idea is to let each team member see how the rest of the team is faring as regards the honing of their skills.

As some team members begin to develop a better game with each drill, the others will also be encouraged to make the same level of improvement in their own game.

The beauty of volleyball tactical drills is that as each team member sees his comrades perfecting their moves and improving their game, he will become more and more confident in their ability to play the ball just right.

And because you are running your tactical drills such that the entire team has perfected their moves, the team will then become more proficient in their plays as one unit.

With enough practice, you will no longer be six players on the court, but one team – one entity out to grab the win.

If tactical drills are done properly, you should expect each player to know instinctively where to stand, how to it the ball, and who to hit it to as an end result.

Each team member will also know exactly what is expected of them such that they can run through their plays quickly and proficiently in an actual game.

Soon, you and your team will reach a skill level you never even thought you could reach when you first began to engage in the sport.

Watching each team member play better and better the more you perform tactical drills effectively builds the team's confidence in themselves.

This is important because confidence can sometimes spell the difference between winning and losing a game.

A confident team is assured that they will play to perfection even before they set foot on the court, and this gives them an edge and increases their chances of coming out on top.

Being confident takes away any apprehensions you may have about any aspect of the game and helps ensure that you can give your all as soon as the game starts.

Volleyball tactical drills are indeed among the most important drills you need to run during volleyball season.

That's because as volleyball players, you should always be conditioned to deliver what is expected of you and to have the technical skills necessary for you to make all of your plays work to your advantage.

Tactical drills will make use of all the training you've gone through so far and put it to practical and effective use.

The more you run your tactical drills, the more proficient, trusting, and confident your team will be and the better chances you will have of winning all of your games.

Part 4
Serving Drills: Fun Ways to Improve Your Skill

Serving Drills: Fun Ways to Improve Your Skill

Serving is one of the most important volleyball skills you need to learn.

You have to realize, however, that serving can be a tricky skill to learn at times.

Fortunately, there are a lot of volleyball drills you can perform to build your expertise in this particular skill.

What's even better news is that aside from being very effective and delivering an important result, serving drills in volleyball can also be among the most fun drills you'll ever have to do.

Remember that volleyball serving drills should be aimed at developing consistency, enhancing accuracy of aim, and increasing power.

A serve is the beginning of every play in the game of volleyball, which is why they should never be taken lightly.

They can, in fact, make or break your chances to dominate and win each play.

For this reason, you have to run the most effective volleyball serving drills regularly to make sure you and your team are always kept in good shape.

To learn the basic skill of serving in volleyball, you would do well to perform the serving relay drill.

This drill requires a volleyball team to be divided into two groups.

Each group shall form a line – one on the left and the other on the right side of the court.

The first person in each line will be asked to serve the ball and then run to the other side to retrieve the ball. If the serve is good, then they are asked to hand the ball over to the next person in line, who then repeats the process.

If the serve is unsuccessful, then the player should keep repeating the process until he delivers a good serve.

The first line to have all members successfully complete a serve wins the drill.

The *Around-the-world Drill* is also a good drill to run if you want to hone your volleyball serving skills.

This drill requires you to divide the team into two groups.

The receiving team will ask one player to sit on a specific area of the court and then the serving team will have to serve the ball to that particular area.

If the receiver can catch the ball easily while seated, the server then moves on to the next area on their side and then the first receiver will now take the role of server.

Each group should rotate until all members have successfully served the ball.

There are serving drills in volleyball that are competitive and timed, such as the *Dead Fish Drill*.

The team is divided into two groups, with one group positioned on each side of the net.

The competing groups alternately serve the ball for two minutes.

If a player serves unsuccessfully, he is asked to go to the opponent's side of the net and lie down, thus becoming a "dead fish."

He can only go back to his own side and begin serving again if a server from his group hits him with a serve.

The group with the most number of dead fish at the end of two minutes loses the drill and the winning group decides their penalty.

There are several different volleyball drills you can perform to condition yourself and prepare for a game.

In fact, knowing what drills to run and how to run each drill successfully is one of the best ways to help your team attain success.

And because the serve is the very first play in any set of exchanges in volleyball, it often sets the tone and pace of the current exchange.

If you are able to control the serve and make it work to your advantage, then you can start celebrating as you and your team start dominating every game you play.

Above all, remember that serving drills aren't just for beginners in the game of volleyball.

Even those who have been playing the game for quite some time still need to continue enhancing their skills to make sure they are always on top of their game.

So, no matter how long you've been playing volleyball, make sure to always work on your serving drills, especially as each volleyball season begins.

PART 5
The Importance of Volleyball Setting Drills

The Importance of Volleyball Setting Drills

The set is considered to be the pivotal play on any exchange in volleyball.

For you to understand better why a set is important, let us look at how it is performed.

The team's blocker digs the ball to the setter, who then positions it to the ideal spot for the team's hitter to get in a successful kill.

If the ball is not set just right, you will not be able to deliver a strong hit, no matter how good your hitter is.

That's why it is very important to run through some effective setting drills regularly.

Regularly running volleyball setting drills will allow your team's setter to master hitting the best ball positioning.

At the same time, it helps build teamwork as the rest of the team encourages the setter to perform his function just right.

Being confident that your setter will position the ball just right will also give the blockers confidence in their own ability to dig the ball to the setter, knowing that it will be well taken care of.

In the same way, the hitters will be confident that they can hit the ball at just the right position that is in their best interest based on the current exchange.

One of the most basic volleyball setting drills is called *Kill the Setter Drill*.

Remember that all players in volleyball are potentially defenders, and this drill is targeted at teaching the setter how to successfully transition from defender to setter and back again.

For this drill, the setter is positioned at the back and the hitter in front.

The coach, or another player, then tosses the ball towards the frontline and the setter runs forward to set the ball and then returns to the starting position.

Once the setter masters this drill, he will be more prepared for the quick change in position that's often required in making a good play.

One of the skills a good setter needs to possess is the ability to see what's happening on the other side of the net while he is setting the ball.

Towards this purpose, you can run a drill called *Reading the Block*.

For this drill, the setter is in position and a player tosses the ball from the other side of the net.

As the ball goes up, the coach or another player makes a hand signal of sorts.

The setter then calls out the signal before setting the ball.

This drill helps the setter develop his observation skills.

There is also another variation of the Reading the Block drill, where a defender is positioned at the centre of the court.

The setter is also in position on the other side of the net.

As the ball is tossed to the setter, the designated defender decides whether to move left, right, or stay at the centre.

The setter has to decide how and where to set the ball such that the hitter can take advantage of where the defender has positioned himself.

An observant setter can set the ball in a way that the hitter can exploit any lack of coverage on the opponent's part.

Running setting drills regularly will provide your setter with the necessary confidence that'll help your team take control of each play and gain momentum each time the ball is on your side of the court.

As with any other game or sport, confidence can spell the difference between winning and losing a match, which is why it is very important to build the confidence of each member of your volleyball team.

Volleyball setting drills also help your team become better organized and better able to deliver more kills on a regular basis.

As your setter becomes more skilled and his reactions quicker, the drills you run will definitely become more fun to execute.

After all, the whole purpose of choosing such drills is to have fun while learning the game and enhancing your skill.

PART 6
Taking Advantage
of Offense Drills

Taking Advantage of Offense Drills

Among the most important aspects you should strengthen as a volleyball team is your offense.

To do this, it is necessary to run effective offense drills as part of your regular training sessions.

These drills are used not only to hone your skills in volleyball offense, but also to strengthen your bond as a team, raise your confidence in each other and the team as a whole, and build a strong sense of trust among the players and the coach.

These factors are important because they are the factors that allow your team to work together as one entity on the court.

Volleyball offense drills help the members of your team develop trust in each other because they are able to witness how each of them begins to improve in the performance of their individual functions.

As they learn instinctively where to position themselves at specific points in the game, how to get where they need to be, and how to control the ball from their end, they will not only develop trust, but confidence in each other as well.

Take note that volleyball offense drills are often very precise, and they teach players to master strong movements as well as ball control.

A pass-set-spike type of drill is one that will help you enhance your movement skills and precision.

However, this drill is a bit tricky to perform.

For this drill, your team has to line up in three rows on one side of the net.

Have the lines start as close to the net as possible.

The drill then begins by having the first person in each row lie on his stomach.

The coach will then stand in the middle of the opposite court and then throw the ball over the net.

As the ball is released, the players who are lying down should get up and run to position themselves.

The player in the middle then passes the ball to the one on his right, who sets the ball to the leftmost player, who then hits it over the net.

These players then move to the end of the line and then the next players in line repeat the process.

The setting accuracy drill is another offense drill that targets precision.

For this drill, the team should form a setting line on the right.

A team member stands on a chair with his arms raised above his head.

The coach will then throw the ball to the setter, who sets the ball such that it hits the hands of the player on the chair.

Each setter should set five balls correctly, with each ball coming from a different angle, thrown at a different speed, and from a different height.

This allows you to master the art of setting to the same spot no matter where the ball comes from and how it is passed to them.

In any volleyball game, accuracy is a very important factor.

To increase your hitting accuracy, you would do well to run the 4-corners drill.

This drill requires you to mark off for sections on the other side of the court.

The player should line up in single file.

The coach then throws the ball to the first player in line and call out a specific section.

The player then hits the ball to the indicated section.

The drill requires the players to think quickly as to what is the best way to hit the ball such as to get it accurately into the specified section.

The 4-corners drill can be run in a variation that'll help you build your skills in volleyball offense even more.

The positioning of players is basically the same, but this time you place an object in the middle of each section on the other side of the court.

The drill can also be made more fun and interesting by providing rewards for each player who hits the object in each section accurately.

At the same time, you can set penalties for players who fail to hit their mark.

Volleyball offense drills are crucial to the success of any volleyball team.

You may have noticed that offense drills are more advanced than other basic tactical drills.

That's because it's essential to make sure your team can successfully execute each hit and play before they even set foot on the court.

The good thing is that you can always modify these drills to suit the needs of your team.

What's important is that you use them properly to strengthen and solidify your team.

PART 7
Why You Need
Defensive Drills

Why You Need Defensive Drills

Volleyball is one sport where every single player has to learn to be both an offensive and a defensive player.

In order to play good defense, you'll have to learn the best way to dig the ball.

For those who aren't so familiar with volleyball terms yet, digging is the act of preventing the ball from hitting the ground on your side of the court.

Furthermore, all volleyball players also need to have the ability to block spikes from the other team and react appropriately to free ball situations.

To hone your defensive skills and get ready for an actual game, it may be best to run defensive drills regularly.

These drills teach you how to dig balls aggressively and train you to anticipate the next move of your opponent so you'll know exactly where and how to block or dig the ball.

There are plenty of such drills you can take advantage of to enhance your skills as a defensive player.

The Jump-to-Block Drill

The Jump-to-Block Drill is one of the most basic defensive drills for volleyball players.

It aims to teach players how to move correctly when digging a ball at the net.

For this drill, the coach stands on a chair at one side of the net and throws the ball from different positions.

The designated defender will have to jump to the right position that's best suited to blocking the ball.

Once a defender is able to block the ball properly, the coach throws the ball to another direction or from a different position.

This may be one of the simplest defensive drills, but it is also among the most important for honing each player's defensive skills.

Touch Ten

Touch Ten is a defensive drill that helps build coordination and anticipation in volleyball players.

It also helps build a player's stamina. This drill is done by having a defender on one side of the court and a setter and three frontline hitters on the other.

The coach tosses the ball to the setter, who sets it up for a hitter to spike over the net.

The defender should make sure the ball never touches the ground.

This drill may require the defender to move around his entire side of the court, since he is defending all by himself against four other players.

The defender may be replaced after he has successfully defended ten balls in a row.

Dig and Roll

Another fundamental defensive volleyball drill is the *Dig and Roll*.

For this drill, the defender should stand in the middle of his side of the court.

The coach then stands on the other side and hits the ball to either side of the designated defender.

This drill teaches the defender to read the body language of his opponent and anticipate which direction the ball will travel.

After digging the ball successfully, the defender will then roll to the right and then get back to the starting position.

This will help enhance your sense of timing and anticipation.

Running a variety of defensive drills for volleyball players will make it so much easier for the team to dig the ball from any direction possible and no matter what the situation is.

And the more you run these drills, the more likely your team will be to develop quicker reflexes and the more instinctive their responses to each play will be.

This allows the rest of the team to know exactly how the ball is going to be played every time.

Take note that a solid set of defensive skills will make it that much harder for your opponents to score and it will be that much easier for your team to dominate the game.

So, the next time you set up a training session for your volleyball team, remember not to concentrate on improving your offensive skills alone.

Defense is just as important and may even be more useful in the overall scheme of things.

PART 8
How to Increase
Your Vertical Jump

How to Increase Your Vertical Jump

Volleyball is among the types of sport that require players to have high vertical jumps.

That's because volleyball players who're able to jump really high are better able to deliver killer spikes and block balls more effectively.

If you are one of those volleyball players plagued by low vertical jumps, then it's about time you considered getting tips on how to increase your vertical jump.

Of course, having a high vertical jump alone does not necessarily make you the best player in your team.

However, by undergoing vertical jump training, you're not only increasing your jump, but improving your game as well.

Having an advantage over your opponent can give you the necessary confidence that may spell the difference between winning and losing a game.

It eliminates any apprehensions you might have because you know that you've trained well and you're at least one step ahead of your opponent.

In your effort to achieve higher vertical jumps, you'll have to work on the right set of muscles.

This will guarantee that you have enough power, excellent reflexes, and a better game overall.

One very effective way to achieve a higher vertical jump is to do squat jumps regularly.

This exercise is done by holding two dumbbells in an upright position and then squatting down gradually until your knees are at a right angle position.

The aim of this exercise is for you to jump from this position at a height of 10-20 centimetres.

The Leg Press
The Leg Press is also a good exercise for increasing your vertical jump.

This exercise begins with you seated on the floor, with your hand supporting your knees.

Make sure that your knees are angled comfortably while you're seated.

Gradually bring your right leg to your chest and then straighten it until it is fully extended.

Repeat the process with your left leg.

You have to make sure that you move slowly and correctly in order to avoid injuring your legs.

Jumping ropes and sprinting are also very effective exercises for improving your skills in vertical jumps.

Jumping ropes help develop your leg muscles and strengthen them.

It also helps you enhance your twitch muscles and increase your foot speed, thus making you better able to jump vertically.

For its part, sprinting helps strengthen your leg muscles so you'll be able to jump explosively when a game calls for it.

Another set of exercises that work really well in increasing your vertical jump is a combination of lunges and toe raises.

These exercises strengthen your quads, calves, and buttocks.

And if you want to bring your leg strength to the next level and make it even easier to achieve high vertical jumps, you might choose to use weights when doing lunges and toe raises because they provide added pressure to your legs and allows you to develop extra jumping power.

As long as you're dedicated and committed to doing the necessary exercises that will give you stronger legs and more jumping power, then you will surely achieve your goal of having a higher vertical jump in no time at all.

You would do well to use a volleyball jump training manual as your guide because such manuals typically contain illustrations along with the instructions, which makes it easier for you to execute the exercises correctly.

PART 9
How to Ensure Serving Success in Volleyball

How to Ensure Serving Success in Volleyball

The serve is said to be the most critical component of any volleyball game.

That may be due to the fact that if you fail to deliver on a serve, your team will surely lose the point.

In the same way, you are almost always guaranteed a win if you constantly ace your serves.

It doesn't even matter if you're new to the game or a professional volleyball player; you have to brush up on serving basics in order to improve your overall game.

In serving effectively, it is most important to master the fundamentals of the overhand serve.

Remember that body position, ball position, arm position, ball toss, and ball contact are all very important in delivering a successful overhand serve.

Your feet, hips, and shoulders should all face the direction where you want the ball to go.

You should also make sure that you hold the ball at chest height and that your elbow is loose and slightly bent.

The elbow and hand of your serving hand have to be at a 90-degree angle, at ear level, with the hand open and the wrist locked.

Furthermore, you should hold the ball in front of your serving shoulder and toss it about 12-18 inches above your head.

Make sure you strike the middle of the ball with the heel of your hand as you step forward.

To guarantee maximum power and velocity, follow through the motion and finish with your serving hand in line with your body.

Some of the most common mistakes volleyball players make during a serve involves a poor toss, a loose wrist or hand, and a lack of confidence.

The most critical aspect of your toss is consistency.

This means you should maintain the same ball position and height with each toss you make.

You should also aim for just one point on the volleyball and strike that point with as much force as you can.

You should also remember to always keep your serving wrist and hand locked and stiff when you hit the ball.

And while practice does make perfect physically, it is confidence that's truly the key to perfecting the mental aspect of the game.

It's important that you run serving drills regularly in order to create consistency in your serve.

You cannot expect to achieve a reliable performance unless you're willing to go through drills on a regular basis.

A good beginner serving drill requires two players to stand opposite each other on the court.

You and your partner will then take turns serving to each other.

Start serving at the 10' line and then move backwards after every five serves until you eventually get behind the baseline.

As your skill level improves, you can try serving from different areas of the court so you can perfect your service placement.

Players who have mastered the basics of a volleyball serve would benefit from intermediate level drills.

The primary purpose of such drills is to improve your accuracy.

For such a drill, you will need the entire team, divided into two groups, with one group on each side of the net.

Place a chair in zone one of each side and then have a player from each group sit on the chair.

Each member of the team will attempt to serve the ball such that the player seated on the chair can catch it.

Move the chair to another section of the court when all team members have successfully delivered a serve.

You should also remember that just like any other sport, your strategy can make or break you in a volleyball game.

A good strategy can build your team's confidence and momentum when executed properly.

And it is best to map out your strategies as soon as all members of your team have been familiarized with the different types of volleyball serve.

Furthermore, you should educate all players on the different zones of the court and make sure that each of you understands the strengths and weaknesses of your opponent.

This is the key to an effective offense.

It may not seem like it, but volleyball is most definitely a physically demanding sport.

It requires flexibility, strength, and power. If you're serious about improving your overall performance, then you should engage in strength training.

This is vital for preparing your for the demands of a volleyball game.

In strength training, you should give particular emphasis to your core strength, which is what facilitates your balance.

By getting stronger, you can start looking forward to playing better.

PART 10
Taking Advantage
of the Float Serve

Taking Advantage of the Float Serve

Volleyball can look like a very easy game to play when you watch professionals do it.

However, learning how to play the sport can entail a lot of hard work.

In fact, volleyball is perhaps one of the most physically demanding of all sports.

For one thing, it is one of the few sports that require all players to be both offensive and defensive players at the same time.

There are a lot of individual skills you need to master if you want to become a good volleyball player, and one of these skills involves serving.

You probably already know that a good serve is critical to dominating a volleyball game.

Well, there are different types of serve and you'll have to familiarize yourself with each of them in order to be truly effective as a volleyball player.

One type of serve that's very useful is the float serve.

It got its name from the fact that a ball that's hit with this type of serve actually floats in the air rather than shooting forward.

The float serve is important for several reasons.

First, a ball that floats is much more difficult to track, which means that it's difficult to anticipate exactly where the ball may land.

This requires the defenders to be on their toes so that if the ball moves towards them, they'll be ready to move accordingly.

Another important detail is that the wind can actually direct a floating ball, so as to drop it in a seemingly random pattern.

It can also be quite difficult for a defender to hit a float ball back because of its lack of spin.

The most important detail you need to understand about a float serve is that the ball doesn't have any spin on it.

This allows the air to affect the ball's course from all directions.

Try to imagine a ball rebounding off a wall without any spin.

This ball will likely follow a path that's completely opposite from the direction that it hit the wall.

On the other hand, if the ball rebounds from the wall with a spin, it often loses some of its speed and bounces back at a different angle.

Understanding the theory behind the float ball lets you know exactly what you would want to accomplish when using this type of serve.

It would please you to know that the mechanics of a float serve are easy enough to master.

You need to stand about a foot behind the baseline with your left foot forward, pointing straight ahead.

Your right foot should hold your weight and should be turned almost sideways.

When you face forward, your body should be at a 45-degree angle at the waist.

Hold the ball at waist level in your left hand and then point your right hand upwards behind your head, making sure it is bent slightly.

Toss the ball just a little over your head, shift your weight to your left foot and then hit the ball with the flat of your right palm.

Be careful to follow through only about halfway.

Reverse the positioning of your hands and feet if you're a left-handed player.

Once you're familiar with the mechanics of the float serve, you move on to perfecting the technique.

Hold the ball such that the air hole is in the centre of your palm.

You should also make sure that you hit the ball only with your palm and right at the centre.

And when you shift your weight forward, you should drag your back leg along the path of your hit.

This helps you guide your body so you're able to hit the ball correctly.

With enough practice, you will soon find it easy to hit a float serve.

This will help you deliver a serve that's difficult for your opponent to return, thus creating an opportunity for your team to score a point without even having the ball hit back over the net from the opposing side.

An effective float serve can often spell the difference between a good volleyball player and a great one.

PART 11
Mastering the
Volleyball Pass

Mastering the Volleyball Pass

The pass is one of the most important elements in volleyball, as it can serve as the basis for excellent setups that allow a team to score.

It is therefore important for your team to have a number of good passers who can effectively take the lead in receiving serves from the opponent and priming your setters for a good hit.

Every volleyball passer starts out by watching the server of the opposing team and learning how to read his body language.

He should observe where the server focuses his sight and be prepared to move to that particular area as soon as the ball is hit.

A lot of servers hit consistently to the same spot, and a good passer is able to take note of this and respond accordingly.

You can give extra coverage to the server's favourite spot while remaining alert and ready to change directions should the server suddenly decide to hit a different spot.

A good passer always knows where his setters are and is always able to get the ball to a setter no matter what the circumstances are.

Even if you have to run to the boundary line to dig a ball that's too close to call, you still have to be aware of your setter's location and be ready to hit the ball to him.

Remember that a pass that's directed properly to the setter makes it so much easier for him to set the ball up for a great hit.

Passers have to remember that they should always call the ball.

This is one element that a lot of passers take for granted.

The sad thing is that when calling the ball is ignored, it can cause a lot of confusion on the court.

As a passer, you should call the ball so the other players will know that they don't have to go for it.

This allows them to prepare for the next steps of the play.

This means the setter and the hitter can both get into position, confident that someone is already working on passing the ball to them.

When you are passing the ball, make sure that your arms create a flat surface for the ball to bounce against.

Your hands should be clasped together so your arms don't come apart because this can result in an illegal play.

Furthermore, you should direct the ball with your body.

This means that you should be facing in the same direction you want the ball to go.

To create the perfect pass, you should get to the correct spot in time for you to plant your feet and position yourself under the ball facing your setter.

You should also remember that a good passer always digs for the ball.

No matter where the ball is coming from, you must be prepared to dig for it from any angle or position.

For this reason, you should always wear knee pads and practice sliding so you're prepared to get underneath the ball at all times.

A lot of serves and hits won't be directed towards your ideal spot on the court, so you must be ready to get on your knees or dive to the ground in order to return a solid pass.

As long as you constantly practice all the essential aspects of a volleyball pass, you'll surely be prepared for any type of hit that comes your way.

Remember, though, that while your team should have specific players designated as passers in the rotation, all team members must be familiar with the principles of excellent passing in volleyball so they can step in whenever necessary.

PART 12
The Importance of a Well-Executed Volleyball Spike

The Importance of a Well-eExecuted Volleyball Spike

Even a casual observer would probably pick up the fact that learning how to effectively execute a volleyball spike is an essential skill for volleyball players.

This may not be an ability that you're naturally born with, but the good news is that it can be learned and mastered with proper training and constant practice.

Approach properly marks the beginning of a great volleyball spike.

The hit begins at a position about three or four strides from the net.

A two- or three-step approach should take you through the entire motion, which includes the reach over and the follow through.

Air spikes should therefore be a regular part of your warm-up sessions, especially if you're still relatively new to the sport.

That's because your body naturally develops muscle memory, which means you'll be able to feel the proper execution of a spike and with more familiarity, you'll be able to experience greater success.

Take note that great spikers are fearless and confident in their ability to hit the ball over and against any block.

There are several options you can choose from in your effort to hit a spike even against a two-man block.

But, above all, you must believe that you can spike over any block the opponent might throw your way.

You have to realize that as the hitter, you have the advantage over any blocker because you can look for holes between the blocks in front of you.

More importantly, you can aim your spike directly through that hole.

Each player on your team can guide you in delivering a spike.

Remember that volleyball is a team game and your team has to play as one unit in order to attain success.

You can ask your team's back row players to tell you if the middle blocker is late in closing because the back row is in the best position to see what's happening in the front row of the opposing team.

For your team to be effective, your teammates should be able to call what the opponent is doing that you can use to your advantage.

One attribute that sets a great spiker apart is the ability to use an opponent's block against them.

This means you don't always have to spike over the block.

With enough practice and skill, you can effectively swipe the ball off your opponent's outside blocker.

This skill makes you a strong point-producing spiker.

Your goal here is to set your opponent's outside arm as your target.

You must then hit the ball hard enough such that it rolls or bounces off the blocker's arm and lands outside the line.

Such a move will make it quite impossible for the opposing team to cover the ball, thus adding to your points and helping your team dominate the game.

The good thing is that all players can learn this skill, regardless of his primary designation in your team.

Tall players or those who are good vertical jumpers are able to make contact very close to the net without reaching over.

If they're fortunate enough not to have blockers in the way as they hit the ball, then they can pummel it straight down for a quick point.

Players who aren't so tall or can't jump so high should spike from farther away.

The mechanics of spiking, however, are the same no matter where you spike from.

The best spikers are able to convert hits into points in a variety of ways.

Remember that good spikes are important because they not only help the team score more points, but also help develop the team's confidence.

As a result, your team has greater chances of winning more games than usual.

Made in the USA
San Bernardino, CA
27 February 2013